FREER

FREER

by

Will Hochman

Pecan Grove Press San Antonio, Texas

ISBN: 1-931247-34-x

Pecan Grove Press
Box AL
1 Camino Santa Maria
San Antonio, TX 78228-8608

Acknowledgments

The following lists the individual publications of poems in this manuscript:

"Sharkboy@Hombre" was published in *Computers and Composition* in 1997; "Jazz Cat Prism" was published in *Buffalo Bones* in 1998; "After An Old Picture of School House Children," "Baby on The Bench," "Little Girl in the Kitchen" and "Star Mill" were exhibited with photos for "The Glass Negative: Under the Sky, Central Colorado" in 1998; "After an Old Picture of School House Children" was published in *In Praise of Pedgagogy* in 2000; "Bears of Cheyenne Canyon" was published in *Grrrrr A Collection of Poems About Bears* in 2000; "In the Ear of the Beholder" was published in *The International Journal of Sexuality and Gender Studies* in 2000; "Tasting Rain" and "The Trouble Tree" were published in *Interpretations* in 2000; "Henry's Jailhouse Recipe" was published in *Radio! Radio!* in 2000; "Hypertext's Absolute Zero, No Return," "Prepositions Painting Lawrence's Taos Window" and "Sea Change Day," were published in the *Connecticut Review* in 2001; "Star Mill" was published in *The North American Review* in 2001; "Hypertext Underwear" was published in *BiMagazine* in 2004; "Freer" was published in *Greatest Hits* in 2004; "Missing The Old Man In The Mountain" and "Poem Only Now" were published in *Connecticut River Review* in 2004; "Waterfall on the Rocks," "Usually Near Dawn" and "Massage the Day" were published in *Clara Venus;* "Smoke in Your Eyes" was published in the *Connecticut Review* in 2005; "Breaking the Sun" and "Ghost Riding at Kicking Horse Reservoir" were published in *Living Waters* in 2005; and "Autumn Grin" was published in *Caduceus* in 2005.

For Jan Spiegel, the love in our lives, and all readers

DEATH IS A FREER AND SO IS LIFE: NOTES ON WHAT THIS POET KNOWS BEST

Freer is a book that collects more than a decade of poetry writing. It also collects itself into a statement about how poetry is a shifting sense of self that transforms place, memory, performance and selves to open doors of perception into a language and life-flow that water may know best, but we may know and feel as well. The book is divided into four sections. Each section refers to a place I've lived because poems can be manuals about how to inhabit varying spaces. The sections may point toward perceptual nuances as their poems let us attune our understanding of common or unusual experience. These poems are my life. Ironically dying could make them better which is just one of the possible meanings Wallace Stevens intended when he wrote "death is the mother of beauty." And I can also imagine J.D. Salinger thinking that publishing poems is a perfect "bananafish" way to kill them. Nonetheless, as they emerge into the light off the page, I hope that letting my poems do their work makes me a freer in as many ways as you can imagine.

"Second Street Metaphysics" is intended to play with the ways metaphysics needs a second street to see itself metaphysically. I also wanted to play with the fact that I actually lived on Second Street between Avenues B and C in New York's East Village. If reality is A, and consciousness is B, then meta-consciousness is C. I believe that how we travel between our own multiple consciousnesses so fluidly is a metaphysical wonder of the brain, heart and spirit that freer poetry knows best. We sometimes overlook those shifts—as if perception was equipped with an automatic transmission. The poems in this section use urban places, varying points of view, and varying styles to sense shifts between reality and imagination, between writer and reader, and between self and inner self

I've lived much of my life bouncing between the east coast and the Rockies. *Freer* fuses the two poles of my locations. If the city made me learn about its metaphysics, the West taught me to write with heart and humor. The mountains there taught me a great deal about light which is a serious thing for any artist, but in my case, the western light danced, joked, and made me love my eyebrows and hats all that much more. I moved to Colorado's Cheyenne Canyon when I left New York in 1991. The memory of my Colorado life mixed with my time living in Montana fifteen years before. The ever burning brightness of the mountain light, particularly at sunset in New Mexico, is the illumination beyond the words on pages of this section. The shadows too.

When I published my first book, *Stranger Within,* in 1993, I composed the final draft on a Macintosh computer. I knew then and know now that computers and the net make reader response criticism far more important than most literary theorists wanted to guess. I embrace online life as a place where writing, reading, and responding are so fluid it's as if electrons liquefy textual transaction almost as naturally as we do in our selves. Computers for me have always meant a better home for a writer's words to live and dance. The emergence of the internet and the collection of this book's poems share a similar time frame. For me, a key reason for good living online is participating on an email list (Crewrt-L) where writers talk. The workshop model is extended by the list beyond the walls of classes into a "salon" of sorts for like-minded artists. Being part of this email list is as comfortable as a couch, and the processes of showing writing and sharing readings with other writers online energizes my imagination. "Living Online" is a section name that hopefully helps to establish hypertext as a poetic fact of life.

The book's final section, "Crossover Lessons from Short Beach" is meant to capture several textures of my life and work. I presently live in Short Beach, a section of a small town on the Connecticut coast. Walking the beach everyday with my dog has taught me to seek the calm of this water with its gentle tide rocking the world of my learning soul.

I have been a writing teacher since 1976 and I've always felt lucky and privileged to do this work. The way I earn my living crosses over quite naturally into the way I live my life as a poet. Though academic words meeting poetic words for me may have started out as a series of conflicts, I simply believe that *Freer* may promote the feeling and idea that creative thinking and critical thinking are really the same thing. That's what my life is really all about. No matter what the context, my work with words is charged with alternating current between the poles of school and art. I think traditional, academic discourse need no longer remain traditional, and I enjoy the way responders to art increasingly become part of it. I embrace multigenre writing and teach it in my composition and creative writing classes. I think my students learn powerfully about "writing as the art of collage" because it shows respect to other writers and their ideas, while challenging students to create new statements and texts of their own. The continuum of poetry, fiction, drama, non fiction, criticism, and metacriticism would be more fluid if we let genre divisions accept diversity and if we try to use collaboration more easily. In other words, now is the time to come together and here is the poetry to be freer.

Contents

Second Street Metaphysics

The Colors of Light on Cheyenne Road

Living Online

Crossover Lessons from Short Beach

Second Street Metaphysics

FREER

I

Not metaphor
Or power
Not author
Or voice
Or character
In you or me
So much as sinew
Legs stretching
Motion
Almost wing-like
And running us
Syllabic perhaps
So toughly loved
And brought
Together word by
Fleshy word, alive
With the fear of crossing
White space
Step by terrified step
To arrive
At the wise suspense
Of foot bridge wood,
Always questioning when
Step will or word
Might break
Across the span
Of our human abyss

II

Imagining a snap
That is jazz
Improvising essences

Seen so clearly,
It seems easy
To become us
Back lit lovingly
With music's intuition
Words smoothly
Fall into sound
Then read safely
Down from beyond
A spine's breaking point
To the place where peace
And synapse conduct
Symphonies

III

So autobiographically
We grow refined
Constant and solid
Like a nerve's sheathing
More viable
Instantly stable
Yet not guessing
The messages deep inside,
The finally liberating story,
The one where death
Is almost sexy...
Maybe this broken
Moment's trance
Will reach out then, laser
Printing imaginary winds
Of love flying
Perfectly puckered
In gravity's last kiss

DOGS IN HEAVEN

Nothing hidden
about them,
no wings though.
Maybe it's more like holes
inside holes, and you
threading selves
through self?

Here, barking is holy
as though seeing
with a needle's eye,
as though freedom
is even more than flying,
as though no eyes
die but go
where vision goes.

THE ART OF COLLAGE IN CRACKED ITALIAN

This little tile,
a reject from its makers
(one of many
from generations of Rampinis)
transcends borders and time
with its cooked sand and color
almost living and grouted
into the jaundiced skin
and coagulated blood
of an Italian family's
dead ancestors.

This particular square
of hand-painted tile
cheaply brought its
right angling of yellow,
green, brown, orange and blue
back from Radda, Italy
(a happy place
despite its sound)
to cast "Il Volpe—The Fox"
stirring in front of a cypress tree,
painted perhaps out of scale
but almost perfect
for all creatures
to see beyond.

The animal's brown pose
and memories of Italy
warm slowly with
tea brewing the green taste
of earth's surface on this tile
cracked and cooling
until it seems to taste
its gaze in yours.

"The fox knows many things,
the hedgehog
 knows one big thing"
the swift worker
may have thought
as he exiled the flawed tile
just past the furnace
to land on the last table
marked even in English,
"Reduced"
and "No Return."

Broken heart dancer
from mold to fired moment,
these ceramic words
are really all of me
cooked, coming apart
and together again,
broken beautifully
to take stock
of me
and think myself
more of a hedgehog
while knowing foxes
(like collage)
import better art.

SUGAR SHOES
for Ed Meek

There are no altars
In this holy pose,
Just toes dancing

I belong where we move
Layering moxie
Cushioning
On top of soles
Scamming selves
Honey-wise and
Accelerating
To whatever sweet
Speeds are needed

Every pair the same
Strange lacing
Of hearts and minds
Against tongue

Smoke In Your Eyes

Remember Tommy and Jimmy Dorsey?
One living in New York and one in Chicago
but both playing work and fate well enough
to occasionally meet up with each other, even here,
even now.

After breaking up their band, the brothers
in their own music would still meet in small towns
along the way to smoke Cuban cigars
almost like smoking their past, fading somewhere
between the more important notes in their lives.

Just meeting then...to listen and maybe talk easily
as if it should have always been like this between them,
just watching the sun sink into increasingly dark
azure shadows before the rising moon shines
its motion and haphazard words into the smoking
that drives them verbally into the glow of concentrated light
like oncoming trains, the light ahead
once brought them closer than they ever really were.

As two middle-aged men may walk and talk,
catch up and let their wry stories innocently
fade into the smoke and decay of the night's maw,
their overcoats and caps guard against possible rain
but become all too stark covers, black against white,
images of a haphazard meeting that fight everything,
even color, into gray submission.

This keyboard tap dancing, this black and white
form of caring years later, even this riff, here, now,
can't stop the all too inevitable swallowing
and subtle grasping of darkness, still wondering
why this acrid tasting kiss of life stays on the tongue,
why such tough smells of our tobacco selves
still signal unknowingly what brotherly touch comes next.

PAIN ILLUSIONIST STRESSES
THE REALITY OF PREPARATION

As if hundreds of knife slashes were salted,
Wounds have their own way of becoming us
Our lip-dry smile and tightening eyes
Only begin the jeering
That further sees in souls the deeds
This unkind mirror must expose

Sometimes, hurting wipes its own memory clean
Like chalk gone gladly bad on a dull black board
Some pain ensures other pain is successfully forgotten
Nevertheless every second of our human lives
Hooks personal worms like gut bait somehow
Slithering to be caught beneath these bleeding lines

Enough skin blunts any knife edge but not blood,
Not today, I'm my own adultery, even I
Don't want to be with me—so I scream inside
To silence my skin from crawling away in shame
And I see inside my closed eyelids
Just enough to sleep this face off

Usually Near Dawn

Beneath sheets and blankets
when not quite done with sleep
but done, something in you
wants for the day of work
to dissipate but you churn
and with eyes consciously closed,
you watch thoughts
silently self-agitate
into tiny, iridescent bubbles
of what might have been.

Past the point of no-return,
the soupy soul in your bowels
crawls into a surviving coil
and spins you into your shell,
a spiraling as inevitable
as the breakfast table.
You step down stairs
with dreams still receding
and think about the toast
browning as you grab
the coffee pot
to test the strength of grip
like a trapeze act.

Postured right, your upstanding,
on-the-level persona
blends self-made moments
with lazy little wishes
spreading dainty thought wisps
and leaving your inner gaze
to turn your fear of wages soft,
as you lick the butter salve
from your lips before going.

MONDAY
for Marc Rabinowitz

Waking up is bad enough,
but having to jack up a car
with dirty white collar hands
and stubborn lug nuts
(whose rust mocks weakness)
was almost too much
until the wrench turns
their hurting into turning,
though this sidewall victory
is not enough to begin working
—black coffee must still kick in.

Reverse turning the lug wrench
to a point still under warm covers
won't work but it does help
to remove dead rubber
looking like a "D"
and standing on its flat side
as the beginning
of a four letter
wake-up sentence
drones me into action:

D-crank-jack
o-crank-jack

i-crank-jack
t-crank-jack.

The spare, after all this cranking,
is flat—there's nothing left to do
but put the flat back on,
jack down and drive

on bad rubber and rim
to the nearest gas station
where a fellow with
"Fred" sewn on his shirt
fixes my struggling without
fearing what is trapped
in his fingernails
and believing that fixing
is simply a matter
for the right tool.

My failed hand twinges
from thumb to wrist
as my fingers keyboard
my reaching and wandering
with an online purpose
that deflates what living
should have been,
turning this torn-carpal day
into the ongoing pain
of my life sentence
about an extended heart line
grease stained into my palm
and linking Tuesday's fortune
to new tread.

STOPWATCH

The world ends with your mother
Calling you home from street play
Or sending you to school days with lunches
That feed love for a lifetime until lost
Between peanut butter and jelly.

So much hope in a sandwich and nothing left
Except perhaps a crumb at the corner of mouth.
With Main Street almost empty, you stand
Beneath a street lamp glaringly mad, angry
At game-ending memories that are hazy now.

Life force is something we give each other
Every day, in small ways, for human and haphazard reasons
Computed as this inevitable give-and-take
Into a quantifiable force that is really the gravity
Of Mothers nurturing beyond their time.

Hotel Allen Ginsberg

for Marvin LeBof and Arthur Adelman

No reservations needed and
Bongos in every room, man

Dictionaries like ice machines
To cool the cool, play the fool

Words do that to us all;
Door keys, checkout time

And life stained rates
On the back of every page

CORRECTING THE LENS
for Bill Sheidley and Seymour Glass

Glass yogis came courting white-turbaned clouds
chanting aloud to weather balloons
in wind rhythms and testing the gravity of their tunes
with holy erotica singing smart eyes home.

Some poets live moments so alert to portals
they illuminate all who pass through on their way
to thumb the soul's dictionary with a strum of words.

Chords and saints live ages apart, alert to dumb horizons
sometimes winging spirits beyond the atmosphere,
though without ground clearance their flesh is telescoped
instantly into a truth sung best only after death.

Maestro, where's the man? Where are the simple hopes?
Not those glory dreams that use gray temples
to make steeples pose perfectly beneath blue skies,
but the ones posturing all people with 4/4 time,
the ones everyday paying humility dues,
the invisible ones dreamed with hearts prayed in full.

IN THE EAR OF THE BEHOLDER
Tipton played as a man for years...

Wrong notes
are impossible
to perform
her fluidity
of a searching
tongue
improvises
perfectly
with the Jazz song
of Billie Tipton
who played opposite
sex so well
five wives
decades
of audience ears
and a stripper
couldn't tell
all but knew
down
to the ivories
touched
and reeds
Billie blew
that Jazz
harmonies
and leads
fingered
in soul
came also
from inner
hopes

playing
humanly
beautiful
into Tipton
from muse
to musician.

SALINGER'S HAIKU PHOTOGRAPHER, ANTONY DI GESU
for Tim O'Connor and Bruce Mueller

The publisher said
The author was on his way
Here and might be shy

Over and over
My white walls imagine color
Smiling at the thought

New shadows emerge
From corner eyelids creased
Expecting his edge

Alone in moments
Before the subject arrives
I welcome his gaze

But polite smile
Gives no texture to frame lips
Against his speaking

My eye in the lens
his black-hole stare won't flinch, break
or give this a chance

I move the angle
Profiles use noses well
Still, he shifts to less

Guessing his smooth flesh
in morning light means to kiss
paper, but with words

I hand him *Catcher*
(I should have had him sign it)
and a coffee cup

He trembles a bit
Sips, lets the book slip aside
Rigid in my eyes

Moving just slightly
Sadness following downward
He stares at his shoes

Before leaving
His face almost said he knew...
So his glance seemed

A good lens must curve
He wouldn't, so no photos
Published from his film

Except memory
The book he touched that day
Grabs me by the soul

Black and white facing
Fear of growing up and old
He knows us too well

Many years later
When I mention Salinger
Without the photo

Young folks know the pose
My flashback makes it certain
Eyes will open wider

GENESIS 9/11

Trade towers for a word
where terror is not Babel

In our darkest moment
let those heroes be us all

Strong beyond the call of war
standing small and remembering

Our falling feet and toes
among the lost shoes

Those tower floors crumbling
too sad in their pull

Of body parts and tears
to want not to die

Against each grain
we lean together still burning

Upon ancient volcanic surfaces
forever crusting a new world

LIBERTY

for Don Anderson

That our laws
Must hold lovingly
And fairly,
The way a white line
Will divide a road
And the way black
Divides white on a page.

Liberty like parallel lines
Meeting somehow
To bend the universe
Into a calm, syllabic revolution
That is always alive
With growth and decay.

All of our atoms
Are one planet
Turning us toward
And away
From each other,
Freer to split the wood
Of ourselves into logs
Splinters, paper and everything
In between

THE COLORS OF LIGHT ON CHEYENNE ROAD

Bears of Cheyenne Canyon

This October a host of silent bears
has come to Cheyenne Canyon
like never before.
Tonight's canyon bear almost looks like
Miles Davis from his *In A Silent Way* days
—black face, black eyes, brown skin tints
and a black mass surrounding his huge,
shiny head, making it appear
as if the bear had some *Round
Midnight* riffs in his walking away sound,
as if Miles with his late night horn
was playing rhythms endlessly
into this mammalian's dark
dancing path of experience
and crossing sounds of the night
into sentences
before ears or bears
know best where to bend.

Even this sleepy, city kid
can watch those quiet
lumbering swatches of huge darkness
kindly cross his asphalt street.
In their hungry-eyed stares of wonder,
he thinks these creatures could eat him so easily,
though they want only to rifle and gobble garbage
and amaze us with their ghostly humility
of what the hibernating winter in their blood
needs to become--some dreaming scene
of humans lumbering away, walking
on their tongues and tasting
the truth of earth.

GHOST RIDING AT KICKING HORSE RESERVOIR
for Dick Hugo

Etched in the rock face
Of your final, falling grin
Is the hoof-to-stone-to-air sound
Wet echoing the paradox
And gravity of kicking
Gravel and ground,
Slimming the narrow rim
Too high above the reservoir.

At horse level
And with self respect
Ready to snap like lost reins,
You listen and hear
Your last thought's words
Like an echo
Before silence
Makes certain
Knowing wind
Means surviving
What death knows
About time.

Don't trot by without
A glance beneath
To the thirsty word geology,
Drowned among kicking horses
Now knowing the wet,
Money truth
Of future development,
Now knowing the reservoir
Damming death
Like home.

Breathe closely
In one-lunged moment
For the other to see you
Struggling for reflective air
In a line's motion
Wrangling real music
From wind beyond
Your own submerging.

You ride
Like a fossil's partial recording
Of some horse-like dinosaur
Topping the geologic charts
With a rocky sound
Rhythmic as the breath
Of human afterthought
And seismic as love.

The Trouble Tree

The story goes
he comes home
each night and hangs
his troubles
like clothes
on the branches
of his hesitation.

These days it's not
war that causes
his twigs to bend
but his brother,
their fist-in-face
voices on the phone,
their wrong silences
and how far they
stretch between poles

What can brothering
mean to these two,
the only two
so different
that to name
their link
a new language
would only be
the beginning?

Underground
is a root system
secretly guarding
and connecting
inverted forests
with emotional foliage

and a water system
thicker than blood.

Deeper still
a wasteland
of wanting
consumes
with emptiness
what generations
meekly inherit
as human nature.

How he sees
into his brother's
core is a gaze
skinning bark
on this tree's
lowest branch,
testing wood
and age rings
until the earth's
true center
is rooted.

Star Mill

Clouds swirl in,
their screen changes
light, creates static
while suddenly siphoned
wind spills into
the spinning eye
of a still-working
windmill somewhere
in central Colorado.
The gust accelerates
creaks into shrieking
until orange sparks
make you almost
believe this weathered
pain generator will stop
turning its blood rust
around your shackled wrist
and wake some stellar
inner-mechanism arising
to compass the night frenzy
of your circling fury
and point reflexively
with prairie fingers
that blade living
into the light we are.

MISSING THE OLD MAN IN THE MOUNTAIN

Granite breaks in a rocky face
Winds scowl and crease the loosening cliff
With the loss of self
The gray memory chunk falling
You would have liked most
Was when Willy and I detached
Throwing caps and gowns aside
We literally howled
With wolves done throat teaching
Human cubs new to the pack
And new to this particular twilight

Howling larynx sounds
Howling nasal knowledge
Howling spirit membership,
And howling safely
From Allen Ginsberg's
Holy ground,
Remember us now
Holding onto every fine mind
For every word's sake

Don't worry though
Our growling
And snarling now go
Where the inverted sky
Glows for us all

Full moon ahead

Henry's Jailhouse Recipe

For love, heat a stone in a stove
until the direction of smoldering
skates blue pleasure striking flint
quietly enough so that sparks fly
skyward, mistaken for stars.

Love is sneaky, dancing on peripheries
worse than drunken pixies stomping all night
on convict floorboards until that someone's
ceiling gives way, but there love is, just
before the cops arrive.

Only with narcolepsy can sleeping
in jail feel absolutely neutral—perfectly
at peace with artistic shifts between dreams
and schemes—but tonight even jail's sweet security
can't sweep love's arty eye-lashing aside.

A painter's default mode for too much red at any age
is never to admit it until integrity's big mouth blasphemy
sinks crimson into skin pigments desperately grasping
what flesh painting flesh must hold holy, wave,
and then let flow at the tip of a dream brush on the wall.

Later, after bail, a girl in a blue, Buick convertible, top down
swoops in performing the pick-up with artful double parking,
brakes screeching, and pausing sweetly enough to let Sam Cooke
begin the radio party by driving love all night long to a point
where wind, music and moment lose all legality.

Massage the Day
for Tia Ballantine

From a stranger's well intended touch
to footprints pounded into red dirt,
Hawaii lives with the lava
that flows from our hard
knowing about the geology
of brother and sister rocks
coming home again and again
to burn paradoxical life and ash
into spectrum seas that get closer
and further from land all the time.

The current sweeps around us,
hugging us beyond shells of self
to accept the breaks and grace
that water knows wind best.
Gabriel Garcia Marquez, tell us
if you will, what these tropical,
proximal bird calls mean,
what the clouds tell the wind
to say to tree branches,
and how the fragments of us
become smoother together.

Though not yet true, tell everyone
and the one soul we sleep nights of life in
just why at Kona sunrise this paradise
aligns with human wave rhythms
...and all that seems to be. Dive, dream
and something whole beneath all surfaces
may be pointed to.
How else can our fingers penetrate
this moment's skin
without our touching,
loving every inch of it?

LITTLE GIRL IN THE KITCHEN

Her image crawls out from emulsion
under the glass negative to clutch
her dolly and offer love that bare walls
and an empty cupboard don't.
Her eyes (a constant blur beyond hope)
won't look to nearby Colorado mountains
for gold, at four or five she's already
clouded and sold into her coal dust life
—she knows no way for Daddy to move
but down, digging black ground deeper.

Those 1913 Ludlow miners struck
for ten cents more a ton, hourly pay
for dead work, for their own weigh men,
and for just a slim chance out from under...
By 1914 grimness had gone beyond
cave-ins; miners and militia fought
in Ludlow's high plains, tent town
where 900 men, women and children
were jack-hammered into death's ore.

Colorado's gray clouds today
find shapes almost like the dolly,
and almost human in their above
ground moment of holding on.
But the pain that burns these clouds
into life is a Colorado strip mine,
plowing under the photo sensitive grave
of this never-rescued girl, her gray rainfall
now our only prospect.

Baby on the Bench

for Jenn Gutierrez

Standing like a bird
on some life wire
and in the background
climbing in all directions
ladders point
beyond the horizon
with loose wood
in the foreground
still building
something more
of our gravity,
our flesh rising
from this bench scene
like some clue of
what all life is made of
at its smallest moment
and spewing
the very material
aura of a standing infant
his sun lighting
the background
of all great
plains and scenes
his lumens
pioneering this space
with love and wanting

Oh baby
your gray overalls
oh baby
your white arms
oh baby
your gravy future

posing
oh baby
your slanted
shadow face
into the eye
of the camera
oh baby
into those storms
of all you will become
oh baby
my baby

Me lifetimes
later photographically
sitting now on the same
bench still squinting
through glare
and smudging
gray tones onto pages
that feel like bench slats
pushing flabs
of my age curved back
between wood and dying,
this snapshot no outake
as it shoots a bull's eye
with memory
curing age

Notes Posing for Georgia

In New Mexico you don't open
your door wide until you know
who's out there--but come in now,
through the courtyard door
at Miss O'Keeffe's hard packed adobe
home in Abiquiu--it will do
for what you need to get a sense
of background, foreground,
and help to frame her paintings too.

The ghosts she housed in adobe
among roof wood called "vigas"
and "latillas" pose Sistine-like
among twigs in their imperfect
right angles while just beyond
countless angels dance
partnering with the shadows
of the thick Spanish walls
called "tapias," and "Tapia"
I am told was also what
villagers nicknamed Miss O'Keeffe's
place before they saw her paint
their land anew.

She saved herself
with each brush stroke
stretching canvas boundaries
"techadito" style all the way
to her Ghost Ranch and beyond.
I had to ask the tour guide twice
how to spell "tech-a-di-to"
(adobe slang for small overhang)
before she explained
it wasn't really a word,
not one I would find in a book.

WATERFALL ON THE ROCKS
Not this dividing and indifferent blue
—Wallace Stevens

We've seen taller
water with better color
and current
with more vigor,
he thought.

We've known white falling
far more fantastically
whorling fury
and carving us into rock,
she thought.

Rocks square geology
with his worn down geometry
of how flow works,
knowing much of her reaching
as a silent question
increases in her head
and pounds tons
of water and rock
into gravel answers
eons after the feeling fact.

A very furry squirrel
in the next moment
crosses mind with nuts
and crackling shells that
automatically link the being's
gray to water sounds
and all that surrounds,
unconsciously of course
our disjunctive senses
work this way.

Trees reach for all
that the sky knows is better,
they beckon farewell and drink her
droplets of river paradox
just to survive.

No waterfall on the rocks
the couple think as they swirl,
falling themselves forever
together in their blue eddy
of saying.

Prepositions Painting Lawrence's Taos Windows

Too chile hot these framed glass windows
Make mountain cliffs ache to fall before rain

Curly purple sage pigments dot the floating landscape
With nurturing figments not imagined but planted

In circulating air embracing red dirt clusters in a grasping
Of motion knowing the earth is hot, and sensing an atomic come-on

That explodes alive with molten morphing and a fire burning below
Fusing New Mexican landscape into color's wordless kingdom

A sunflower's amber molds heat into gold's tawny truth,
A poppy's petals becomes the red legend of Mable Dodge

Water rules and is the color of everything and nothing,
While turquoise tries desperately to cool Lorenzo's flailing

Into swimming oceans of light, into rhythmic attempts
At speeds of love a heart can stroke a brush to

Dark Side of the Door

for Eleanor Popper

Maybe it's the light
I'm finding
hardest to leave,
dressed in Harris Tweed's
best green farewell coat
with hints of rust
threaded so perfectly
that brown buttons
mushroom from the coat's
dense, wooly earth
which grows underground,
yet connects
(stylistically at least)
with a yellow scarf reaching
like a long finger nerve
directly pointing
into an unconscious
part of the skull
which shivers up my own image
in the last steps of two black boots,
departing. I see their heels
glinting and flickering
from a votive candle,
the one that burns
every time death clothes
get tossed my way
and I wear them
for the memory mirror
where I wear
the hats of all fathers
and pull their brims
closer to my face,

hinging each day to wind
and something else,
something close,
something only here now,
something almost resplendent
when leaving yourself.

LIVING ONLINE

Hypertext's Absolute Zero, No Return

Start with zero
Arithmetically when you get
To the end of the story
O. Henry
You'll show
Percentages perhaps
Good enough for tipping
Icebergs.

Otherwise you don't know
From nothing, not even
How zero really works
Or where it sets and hops
Bunny-rabbit cute
Between numbers and letters
With curves almost stalled
Zero Zen, four pawed.

Too lost to find your empty
Self absolutely in the first place,
You hop mostly moment to moment
Zero-multiplying
Koans to realize finally
How harsh facts
Can never count you home
Until you are not there.

THE LAST KEYSTROKE

Once some
metaphysical laptop hacker
beyond all passwords
decides to marry and build a family
(as the security expert
he thinks he will become)
he will read help wanted ads
screen after screen after screen
sweating the me-Tarzan-you-jungle-routine
but this August noon knows better
as the colored light from cobalt
glances through the stained glass
over his right shoulder
into light that seems
to freeze frame the periphery
of this pastiche filament
illuminating his cool burning
in fragmentary moments
so haphazardly azure
that the inner voice in him
couldn't possibly help
but command that he
follow this horizon light
inside all eyes to equalize
their working pressure
like twin earths,
blue, wobbling, and fluttering
with cosmic vision
seeing and screening
their interior colors
so blindingly
they slice tiny edges

of possibility with precision
as his self vision shrinks
to him reaching for a rack
of default blue for his wedding suit.

Hypertext Underwear
for Jonathan Alexander

Despite elastic material
Showing just enough
Anywhere in the world,
Was there the slightest chance
To dress you freer
From academic pinstripes
Here? (Is "click here" now a cliché?)
(Is being free less certain all the time?)
Whatever it is, here won't match
Your screen's customized
Purple zoot suit of flashing pixels
With cool, yellow dots dressed perfectly
For all virtual occasions.

On this planet of pain we drift upon,
You who use ennui as a life-long network
To rightfully seek the holy open source
Of anything, you know who you are,
Pattern setters for clouds,
Ready made for cool,
And fitted with live-in ideas,
You who sweat exuberance juice
Easily and sweetly,
And you who love to jump out of words
(And skin every now and then)
(Crotches linking
What we're really thinking)
You who never forget
About the sexy parts,
Your blood beat is now
Translated into new codes,
Eyes bulging, slashed-open pupils
Admitting an improved ratio

Of more color and feeling
Per thought,
Possible now because
Your hands rip into
Keyboards and screens
With human electricity emerging
So naturally, so purely,
That all garments
Must go

SONOLUMINESCENCE

Start daily with darkness.

Dreams concoct us
And leave the nocturnal
With a not so subtle
Big bang alarm
To ultrasound wake us
From whatever underground
Rooting is now forgotten,
Trouble covers gone,
Bye bye chaos, hello dawn.

Shaking out those creaks
From tired horizon bones
And scraping sleep from wooly teeth
Is like plowing cultivated rows.

Our too human, vibrating mouths
Pound the talked fury of daily duty
Into a very scientific
And utilitarian flashing
Of unlimited potential.

We need only a nanosecond
Happening between sound and sway
To cold fuse life's hydrogen
Into light so sweet
It could invent this sunrise.

Sound now word flowering.

SHARKBOY@HOMBRE

for Dr. Douglas Dieterich

I probably live best
On email these days
I don't live wonderfully
Otherwise, I just feel
Victimized by my liver
(pollution)
And not doing enough
(beyond couch and screen)
Except I do go on
Appearing neatly at work
On working dawns
Each and every week
Almost swimmingly.

Like my father,
I'm not really the hombre
With technical hobbies...
And like my brother,
I'm not always enough the sea lover...
Yet like my mother,
I swim with my heart anyway,
Why not cry my family
Electric into your own
Oceanic reply?
Maybe I'm more than just some modern
Sharkboy ranching fishy lines,
Maybe I'm someone to chum with email
For those ripe online remarks
To stake your sick posts into
With fences like nets to follow.

ONLINE LEARNING
for Mike Palmquist

Take authority for these words
But first trouble the word "authority"
Disregard the sign on every school wall
("Interpretations and checks are non-negotiable")
To meander with thoughts
Through screens trick flickering
Murderous glimmers of having inhabited
Too much authority a little too reluctantly
Turning it into something nuanced
And living well enough to generate human energy
Alternating its current with authority and collaboration
To the point where teaching writing
May mean something more than two
Syllable sides firing ideas at each other,
With tongues and keyboards
Tapping and slapping us all around.

Radically individual authority is a lone ranger
Where electronic context rules like a lecture
With links as silver bullets shooting to the rescue
Of schools where ranges of truth roam
To oppress the home of knowing,
To offer something like safety, something not even
Needing to be said bravely, something like
Authority revealing itself as an ancient mask
Until the piercing glares of future pixels
Force false panaceas to shrink
And reason rides to the rescue
Shooting our dead words
With new responsibility to hear
The lost child cries from all mothers
Nurturing the net's absence as love itself.

IN AN MLA SESSION KNOWING BOOKS ARE DEAD

The noise of a bagel emerging from a brown bag
Wakes me up simply wishing to sip my coffee
And munch some crusty taste of heaven
But no walls will muffle the crinkling of paper
And academic rage in this room.

Poems and good people probably departed
Before this speaker rooted into the podium
And cleared his formal voice to begin
By quoting Thomas Mann:
"We are at the beginning of that which has barely begun

to begin." I'm still waking from last night's
Narcotic logic where clouds stormed their black history
Into my dreaming head, ripping apart the angel of me
And feathering the wind with my schemes of seeding
Minds with words beyond book covers.

Sitting in this folding chair creasing me between
Hunger and listening, they say the internet
Was the hoola hoop of the 90s while my gut knows
It's the feedback loop of life with words often more
Eclectic than what's recycling here as "modern language."

Doesn't it always come down to life being
Disappointing and wanting to use words
To make the disappointment into something else?
Maybe something like butter for the bagel sinking
Into an empty stomach and reappearing here, screen wise

To surprise the daylights out of these dark scholars
Who surmise that youth today don't read but need
The perfect binding of wrong books to love their pages;
I pop the paper bag loudly, hoping noise, mind music
And greasy pixels get me ejected the hell out of here.

Tired of Writing

I've needed a nap
Since waking up today
But there's no hammock
On my horizon
No give on gravity's strings,
No music or kite
Play in my wind

I try to imagine
A lady wearing only
A phony mustache
And broad brimmed hat
Naked and vague
I take her

When I turn her inside out
She's really
A stylish commercial
That wakes my TV sleep
So what? The screen
Keeps wise cracking
24/7
What was I expecting?
Naked poetry?

Conscious or not
Like the mystery
Of soiled sheets
And ink
I want to become
Some
One
Loving each syllable to death

But all that's left is word gravy
Something almost smooth,
Embracing
Then smothering
The eyes-closed taste
Of self swerving silently
Between the dark
And bitter bits
I'm dying alive
Between tasting
Too many sour words
And the point way back
Where my mouth
Best knows taste
Chomping in its own
Uncorrected
Bite

Heading somewhere else,
Like nothing in the evening,
This rudder tongue curls up
In a casket of saliva, enamel
And not very pink gums
To head toward sleep and silence
And float my snoring away
From any rocks of inky angst
With only the black taste
Of my own faltering sound,
Lonely as a foghorn,
Losing to this constant
Shroud of words
Surrounding my opening
Like lips

AMONG THE LAST BOOKS IN A USED BOOK STORE

Get your head exploding sense
Out of the way
But of course you can't
Light hurts, sound hurts,
Words bounce hard off surfaces
Effective or not,
Echoing what's left behind...
The musky, thudding,
Day-to-day
Forgetting that ticks
Like a clock
From the inside out.

This self-reflective light
Glares intensely as the syllables flail
and Espresso with aspirin kicks in,
Book-rowed silence softens something
Just enough to spot another *Neuromancer*
(The last one lost because it was loaned)
For sale, cheap on a cultivated
Shelf if this head pressure
Will just stop the pain
From squeezing eye sockets
Long enough to read
A lightly penciled price.

Storing this moment for lines later
Takes being heroic, staying
Bookshelf sturdy,
Strong, stoic, aware that a red heart
Pulsing black words costs
Something beyond
Rare book value,
Even with original dust

Jacket intact and the book,
Inscribed with whatever
Visceral signature,
Keeps your searching eye
Dedicated to entwined rhythms
Of dead trees singing hymns
Snuggly inside and dancing
With all the right angles.

Blood, nerves, brain cells,
What flows in those hurting
Word channels
Won't stop crushing temples;
Like Anne Frank's Diary,
Your book's spine is worn from
Bending over to pray,
Creasing now at the slightest
Eye contact, every page
Fading with a Nazi glance.
Isn't it sickening how ink
Infects minds into a plague of words
Professing the grave
For good reason?

Cranial grit
Oyster pearl,
Same shit,
If sleep doesn't delete
Senses soon,
Drill a small hole
Emergency style
To stop this screwy rage
Going against the grain
And creating shame.

Living for years
In every second,
Again and again,
No memory,
No chance of escape,
Eyelids, eye lashes, ear drums,
No sense is free from pounding, please
The keys to leave
Are clearly needed
With this page a shade past evening,
Its asylum darkening.

CROSSOVER LESSONS FROM SHORT BEACH

AFTER AN OLD PICTURE OF SCHOOL HOUSE CHILDREN
(When they paid teachers with livestock)

Attending cures snobbery and mind
like bacon, the insufferable arrogance
of ideas exploding in the finally
understood guidance of a storybook pig
who ultimately teaches reading
to generations of prairie kids
frying in the beautiful
unconscious fat of no TV.

So much surrounds this shack
that isn't there—in a picture
tube of time swirling like cotton candy
I see something almost escapable,
something slight, a sliver of students
as young eye glasses
to see school through brightly,
and maybe magnify learning's focus
so much later in their lives.

The camera can't gather their gazing,
and their gleaming faces don't make it
any easier to imagine me the teacher
clicking, clucking, then reprimanding
the memory lovingly, with arms still akimbo.
So much grows beyond the frame
it's fruitless for this humble idea
orchard to expect a harvest sweet
enough to provide anything beyond
the point that there could have been more,
and surely was.

SEA CHANGE DAY

Not a condition, sure
they simply call it
old skin, so Sylvia said,
a grandmother many times
as she rubbed her arm
and her flesh crinkled
as she gasped a bit,
so I should know by now
she continued, walking calmly
by the shore of her age,
her laugh said bruises and beaches
are old hat, but after tonight's stride
it was the windless cove of her gaze,
a strange knowing,
they call it almost sleep, she said,
with torn crags and dark sand
only a dawn could love.

Not a cut or break like that time
with the lawn mower
when she didn't know
how much hand had been lost...
two fingers came up bloody
forever changing the way
grasping works, accidents,
Sylvia said, are only stupid
when you think they won't happen,
and beautifully human
when your luck
sees the healing ahead, yes
human in just knowing
we are still attached, maybe tidal
in our comings and goings, perhaps
earthy in the way two hurt

fingers touch a whole body's pain,
yet somehow we can still make certain
that something holds on
to something more
than flesh and bone,
lost or not.

Autumn Grin

This New England fall
demands color acumen
—yellow, orange and red at least,
to offer the quality of themselves
with brown and black following later
to outline the smiling aperture of anyone
whose open eye and closing pupil
zoom into the security and glare
of peak leaf confidence
lighting a mixture of moxie
and moment that shape something
of self into a brazen assumption
that would be shallow without
those latent shadows
framing dark edges
for this convergence of light
clicking color into earth's skin.

SPEAKING OF EDUCATION
for Wendy Bishop

Most students
as sorcerers' apprentices
learn to become
King Kong academic
language mongers
but only after
wandering jungle lost
in a city of words
and getting shot down
from empire states
of mind with lines like
"it wasn't bullets
that killed the beast,
it was beauty"—this being,
perhaps, a fair sentence
for the crime of loving Fay Wray
which is no different really
than the crime of loving learning
and loving truth
when it comes down to lying
finally silent and dead
on the cold cement of reality
with hardly a crack left
for the magic of illuminating,
one's last moment, almost flying,
ending in a final, learning thud.

John Dewey,
John Dewey,
please put your scarf on
and top hat too
as if Aristotle
had anything on you,

your moments need not
be linear
(or even historically similar)
so much as shared, experienced,
and hopefully understood,
please John Dewey no more thuds,
isn't it true you withstood
school's winter winds
by knowing
throaty, learning-light
glows Whitman-like from within?

The subterranean learning
left here and everywhere
is meaning to leave
with more not less
of self intact, to rage
in verbiage that words
could never simply be,
to find human silence
that is a holy first stroke
and full spectrum too,
like particle and wave
painting learning
as artwork that progresses
until framed alive
(three dimensionally),
if framed at all.

CANCER SCHOOL
for Vivian Shipley

Light so school bus yellow
Its warmth cooks flesh almost
Comfortably with alert color
And orange heat at least
Cooling more slowly
Than bottle glass, possibly made
From batches of this same beach
Sand. Some of those silica grains
Are almost already transparent
Among washed up castles
Of ancient diversions.

Alive mostly in the hazy, imaginary
Burning of human pollution,
As too many thoughts of undone
Classrooms work on the horizon
To invade a mind with incoming minds,
Diverting this joke breaking
Of waves and pleasure reading
To laugh at skin and turn
A teacher's final summer pages
Toward fall and new glass to mold,
When the term is not terminal.

Tired Excited

From too much
Internal rhyme
Or end rhyme
Depending
On the ear
Of the beholder
As I lean closer
To the whisper
Of my own
Poetry fatigue
Missing kissing
But touching cheeks
To listen and hasten
Meaning better
Than sleeping
And then
To finally glimpse
(Red-eyed)
This feeling
Burning me alive
Almost
Like kissing fire

Tumor Rumor

Drink and be whole again beyond confusion.
—Robert Frost

This reach from inside,
Another life aside,
Through crusts of us all
Fingers my unquenchable thirst,
Diagnosed or not,
Earthy, brown and threaded
Iron red with rich blood,
Revealing liver cancer

As pun intended,
As positive test results
Laugh my incarnation
Into a likely last remark,
Alive and dead
With utterance and silence,
A kind of arterial blue
Throbs water and words
Into vast, echoic oceans
Of life and language
Evaporated back again
Through the cloudy carrier
Of this mass inside,
A shining darkness
Like a thunderstorm,
drunk from earthly pole to pole.

In the same cosmic
Gulp of human turning
That lives, drinks and survives
Without really knowing
What this fleshy
Language paddling means,
And beyond bobbing

Tongues that voice,
Kiss, and pause
To give this swim-on sentence
Infusion after infusion
So that this tumor-told fool

Can attune and connect
Beyond surgical visions
Of line left behind,
Beyond life's thirsty literacy,
To somehow live
Beyond the grasp
Of any telling.

House Words

No one ever builds
one house alone anymore,
strangers and nails
must be driven into the grain of it.
Haven't you noticed?
Structure rarely homes itself
to only one piece of flesh
or founding stone.
Time sees to sun
finding windows
no matter where
they are designed,
and along with night
makes certain of desire
(felt or real)
with the deeded decay
and love of black ink.

The rot of the structure
of what one sees
is another building,
altogether unimportant,
though proximal
beyond right angles,
rounding with age
in its faded facade
and appearing to breathe
with a flutter beneath ribs
before falling down
utterly absent
despite decades of standing
up with the false belief,
the hope, really,
that blueprint paper

reverses what lovers
always become
when flesh turns
life inside out.
For instance
I stand here
approximating human skin
that is so easy to fake
it shows the world
how much of me
can stand erect,
metaphysically
together with time's ether,
so well suited
in this sturdy lie
of paint and place.

Roof beams hold heat
high and hard
like clenched fists
hitting a huge forehead
against the days dying
forever in the shame
and shade
of staying inside...

Are scorn and age
a foundation hard enough
to make the concrete mix
with the part of the plot
that finds generations
twisting blood just to live
here?

I can't resist stealing home
away from its typical gaze
with a sly look knowing
whatever dwellers arrive
they mostly live within,
with sad frequencies
akin to hypnotists' illusions,
their fake expectations
commanding my materials
to stay together
for those just passing through.

PLANETARY GRAMMAR
for Christopher Dean

Isn't a hyphen all one needs to join life and language?
It seems absurd at first, but I need something else,
Something I may never know to make sense,
Something proving the earth becomes more choppy,
More talky, and more human all the time.

The ocean of my doubts is not the only ocean.
As land reaches to me with its arms and watery language,
I feel erosion from the point that who I am may work out.
Still stuttering, earth's syllables solidify something impossible,
Something fleshy incorrectly staining the page.

Air, the final silence breathing us, with fire,
Must always and again change things from light to dark;
Their synergy creating sentence gravity, like the comma
Separating "air," "silence," and "fire" just factually enough
To stop words from cosmically becoming their verbs.

JAZZ CAT PRISM
for Steve Rayboy

Ray is not a verb;
I looked it up,
But I swear
I felt some kind of marvelous action
When the last piece of sun
Rayed jazz
Before going down
Like some delicious bird
Whose last flying feather
Fell

It's no different
Than the classic
American difficulty
With death;
There's something
In our national ego
That won't let dying
Encircle us
Without asking
For more time
To improvise a chance
At another verb,
Shining somewhere new
In some other sky

ALREADY MISSING
for Jeffrey Alfier

Fighting poets
Lost in action
Sometimes shop
Meaning, Thursdays,
At the Park Avenue
Stock poetry market
While readers and cigar rollers
Twirl plot twists like this
Into smoke signals,
Knowing their almost
Perfect, momentary
Imaginary work
Must dissipate like ash
Peacefully
Into almost nothing
If not received
With a taste for wanting
Something artfully strong,

Like silence.

Nevertheless,
I'm on a shake, rattle
And roll of snake eyes
And being horrible
To all hearts in general
—You know me
The usual shit sandwich on rye
Writing this original
Thank you note
And sounding like another
Dumb American song
About somebody doing
Somebody wrong

And still somehow
Declaring I belong
Like lettuce, tomato and mayo
Sandwiched atop and beneath
Your overpriced bread.

What a line dance
Of vitriolic, gratitude composing
I'm doing in this million dollar
Home of hosts
To whom I'm hardly
Related with me barely
Weaving thanks in a note or
Into cold conversation
After being fed and given
A hand-me-down
Gray and brown sweater
Made of Icelandic wool
That mustn't be washed,
That was never dyed.
Its rich heritage warms me
In a raw sort of way,
Yet by bed time
I'm wall crawling.

Another upper East Side story,
Not mine, I immediately think
Though not quickly enough;
"Up yours!" the sleepless
Allen Ginsberg in me says
"Up everyone"
I instantly shout back
My light and word-life

Silently frame the dark
For his lion poetry
To shine me brightly
Through the ghost corona
Of a wooly night.

Asleep, finally,
At this borrowed desk,
I want to love and reject
All big-band, one-poem
Money poets
Whose words know
Interest accumulates best
With the right gold, the right
Rhythm and language
Deposited thankfully
Over time.

TASTING RAIN

Youth bends spine to drink
With mouth open wide to sky
Becoming falling

TEACHER OF WRITING

Product
Process
Post-process
Experience pedagogy
John Dewey
Isn't very poetic
(Or at best
Poetic eclectic)
In getting students
To make local
Writing stops
At words
And yet
Diverse minds align

We do prefer
Taking the express
If only thinking
Of saving time
Instead of knowing
Syllabic tickling
Comes from somewhere
Unknown
Between read
And write and beyond
The reach
Of clock
Hands helping,
And hurting
Until the grasping
Comes from the stranger
Within

POEM ONLY NOW
for Dan Spiegel

Lucky in-law
In from the cold
To marry and hold
Daddy's oldest girl
Closer we grow
In Five A.M. hugs
That won't deny
Her father's dying.

Or stop the memory
The request he once made of me
—No poetry please
Over my dead body
This asked to my face
At my own father's funeral
I promised memorably
Never to write
Of my in-law father, the builder
Engineering silence
With structure.

I promised also not to let him
In on my private white spaces
The happy facts
Where dying and poetry go,
Promised not to hammer out
Spirit stanzas
Or lines that craft
With wind
The music of mind.

ON SECOND THOUGHT

Underground root systems
Don't know it all.
Maybe there's more
Of a secret to dying
Than this burial,
The water poet wonders,
Believing secrecy itself
Is always arousing,
Even in blog or wiki.

Amidst the Web's compost
You spread your random seed
And seek moisture beyond
Reaches of time and flesh;
Face it, even dead
You will never rest in peace
Will Hochman,
Why should you?

Whether rocky, craggy or sandy,
The grit of your life
Careened you from mountains
To coast and back again, streaming
Your tears and laughing you
Into boulders and lunar tides,
But hardly generating
The energy of great idea rivers
So much as disorienting
A few uneven lines
Of beach biography

Wounded and crying red,
Your blood deltas itself
Around your thoughts of loss

That feel as life-clogging
As the faults
Humanly stopping you
Every time you try to move
Beyond yourself.

The literacy of your life
Coagulates
Until only a few words
Flow meagerly into
This memory scream,
No flood of language
Comes now to converge
All the veins and scenes
Of anything you have left
Worth remembering.

As if your own river
Knows to forget and flow
Brown, slow and muddy
Into a dirty little marsh
Instead of a true harbor,
You're going where
No good earth goes,
Where caskets don't float,
Where only sinking
And art survive.

You decompose your love
With the very words
That the world has learned
To erode of you through acid
Burning your marble marker
Mistakenly deeper

Into the gray time
Of your life,
Will Hochman.

Unlike the hard work
Of grave digging,
The labors of writing
Are always exaggerated,
Just like your salty story
Of worms and death sex,
You creatively handle
This ground like a stanza.

You are cold now, and dry
Beneath layers of time and dirt,
Almost ambivalent,
Alive only in memory
And in a classic hope that two
Words can find something lost
Of you, so discontent in silica
Grains of ego, your tombstone
Must ask: Another chance?

RECENT BOOKS FROM PECAN GROVE PRESS

Barker, Wendy. *Between Frames*. 2006.
    ISBN: 1-931247-35-8 $9
Byers, Cluster R. *Revisions of Visions*. 2005.
    ISBN: 1-877603-81-3 $12
Challender, Craig. *Dancing on Water*. 2005.
    ISBN: 1-931247-20-x $12
Emmons, Jeanne. *Baseball Nights and DDT*. 2005.
    ISBN: 1-931247-26-9 $12.50
Essbaum, Jill Alexander. Oh Forbidden. 2005.
    ISBN: 1-931247-29-3 $9
Fargnoli, Patricia. *Small Songs of Pain*. 2004.
    ISBN: 1-931247-17-x $10
Haddad, Marian. *Somewhere Between Mexico and a River Called Home*. 2004. ISBN: 1-931247-18-8 $15
Hughes, Glenn. *Sleeping at the Open Window*. 2005.
    ISBN: 1-931247-25-0 $8
Hunley, Tom C. *My Life as a Minor Character*. 2005.
    ISBN: 1-931247-27-7 $8
Kasper, Catherine. *A Gradual Disappearance of Insects*. 2005.
    ISBN: 1-931247-22-6 $8
Kirkpatrick, Kathryn. *Beyond Reason*. 2004.
    ISBN: 1-931247-09-9 $12
Lyons, Bonnie. *In Other Words*. 2003.
    ISBN: 1-931247- 15-3 $12
McCann, Janet. *Emily's Dress*. 2004.
    ISBN: 1-931247-21-8 $8
Mankiewicz, Angela Consolo. *An Eye*. 2006.
    ISBN: 1-931247-33-1 $9
Mohring, Ron. *Beneficence*. 2003.
    ISBN:1-931247-11-0 $7
Pedraza, Venetia June. *Porcelain Dolls Break*. 2004.
    ISBN: 1-931247-19-6 $7
Stryker, Rod C. *Exploits of a Sun Poet*. 2003.
    ISBN: 1-931247-12-9 $12
Trounstine, Jean. *Almost Home Free*. 2003.
    ISBN: 1-931247-14-5 $15

For a complete listing of Pecan Grove Press books and chapbooks from 1987-2006, please visit our web site:

http://library.stmarytx.edu/pgpress